Lois' Little Essays

Lois Vidaver

Front Cover Art by Isabella Foti.

Book design by Mike Miller, pubyourbook@gmail.com.

ISBN: 9781687033604

Dedication

For my four loves:

Mike

Mark

Christa

Isabella

Table of Contents

Hello, there!

Just a word about my journalistic journey...

Deep in my junior year at Hunter College in New York City, I began the semester with a new professor in the Creative Writing department. By then, we students had all been through a course or two: yes, we had scripted a play and plumbed a poem or three.

"For your first assignment in this class," she announced, "I want you to write in a genre you had never tried before. Try something new."

I took the assignment seriously, realizing with a start that I had never written an essay, so write one I would. Opinionated as I was, it seemed a natural. I do not even remember my theme. But I do recall her words several days later as she was returning our submissions.

"I received two essays," she stated, "and they were not good, not good at all." When I look back on it, I distinctly recall, or, given my over-active imagination perhaps, that she dramatically crossed the room and tossed the offending pages into the wastebasket beside her desk.

I got the point. This from a teacher I thought I would like. After all, hadn't she declared on that first day of class that "I climbed into bed last night with John Updike," and gave an impish laugh. Well, did she or didn't she? I had harbored thoughts that this woman had possibilities of holding our attention.

1

So much for getting out of one's comfort zone. Now I was really uncomfortable.

Once in the publishing game, though I worked as a journalist for years, I kept my focus on writing feature articles for newspapers and magazines. Very few essays saw the light of day on my keyboard. Scared away? Youbetcha.

It seemed strange then, that when we moved to Western New York, the "My View" section of the Buffalo News attracted my attention. I grew to look forward to reading those homespun tales of hometown heroes, travel anecdotes, aha moments and family reminisces, all encapsulated in 600 words. They ran the gamut of Life as We Know It.

Being very much up on my venting, pouting, and yes, sentimental skills, I have written and published more than a few "My Views". I even ventured over to other columns where the paper featured "Another Voice", "Women's Voices", and "Viewpoints".

Many times readers press me on whether or not every word I write is true. "Of course," I answer. "Why would I take the time to make things up when real life is so much more interesting?"

It's my story and I'm sticking to it.

Lois Vidaver

Keeping Families Together

"There are some things I'm never going to tell my children."
Lillian of El Salvador

Hurrah! At last, the new U.S. immigration law is working to keep families together instead of tearing them apart. A recent front-page story in The Buffalo News features the story of a young El Salvadoran family—Isaac, Norma, and 22-month-old Joseph Alvarenga. A picture shows them smiling brightly, looking proud. They are about to set a precedent as the first family granted status as legal aliens, even though Alvarenga fails to meet amnesty requirements.

This is good news to those of us in Western New York who have opened our homes and hearts to so many illegal aliens from Central America this year. If there is one thing we can recognize, it's broken and broken-hearted families.

Benedict J. Ferro, district director of the Immigration and Naturalization Service, said that his ability to allow the Alvarenga family to stay comes from his authority to review each case individually.

Hallelujah! May the Service look at every case individually, so that keeping families together becomes its priority.

Refugees by the thousands began flooding into the Buffalo area soon after November 1986 because a new law tightened regulations of illegal aliens arriving in this country after January 1982. Afraid they would be sent home, the refugees were on their way to new lives in Canada, a land with a more liberal immigration policy.

Advocate groups organized carpools to pick them up at the airports and bus stations and bring them to the Peace Bridge for admittance into Canada. But then, on February 20, Canada changed its immigration policies, requiring hearings to process claims for political asylum; refugees were not allowed into Canada until the hearing dates.

Ordinarily, we must admit, Buffalo is not a glamorous border town. There are no stories of people swimming the Niagara River with babies on their backs, or walking for days across Pennsylvania mountains to gain their freedom. Refugees coming through Buffalo—illegal or not—have unobtrusively crossed over one of the several bridges into Canada with nary a nod from a Western New Yorker.

But the sheer numbers of migrants drew our attention. That's when more of us got into the act, offering housing while they were waiting for their Canadian hearings. Families offered to welcome the family groups; seminaries and rectories housed the single men. The visitors stayed anywhere from two weeks to two months.

During that stay time, we began to hear the stories, shocking tales of terror. We heard about war—and what hell it is. We were told about the fear of waking up and leaving your house to find bodies in the streets stripped of their skin. Friends kept disappearing and half a

4

busload of people were assassinated because they had no funds to pay for their freedom.

After she got to know me a bit, Lillian of El Salvador showed the scars running up her arms. Government men held her prisoner for three days, accusing her of helping guerrillas. "There are some things," she said, "I'm never going to tell my children."

The biggest shocker of all is that her six-year-old son Mauricio is with her, but a four-year-old daughter was left behind in El Salvador with Lillian's mother. Leaving children behind? That is inconceivable to me.

But I've never lived with war. It seems that under those horrible conditions—under any conditions—you would take your children with you. But then, I never had to cross the Rio Grande River in the dark of night with water up to my chin—not once, but four times, like Lillian. What would you do with a four-year-old under those conditions? How would you carry her?

Samuel, also of El Salvador, came to Western New York from Houston with an extended family—12 of them. He is bitter. "What this new law does," he said, "is separate families." What he means is, "separate further." Samuel, who came to America in 1978, is eligible to stay in the United States while his wife, who came later, is not. She would have to go back "home" where their two children, nine and 10 years old, are being cared for by her parents. So, in order to stay together, they must pull up roots again and start life anew in still another strange country, even further away from their children.

"Why did you come here in 1978?" he was asked. "That's when the problems in our country started," Samuel answered. "They were taking men to be either guerrilla or military. Didn't want to be either one. They kill people, destroy houses."

If El Salvador is such a dangerous country, I went on, how could he leave his children behind?

"They are safe now," he said. "They are safe until they are teenagers. Then the government doesn't like them. They don't like young people who have new ideas."

Salvadorans Irma and Antonio live with a host family who grew to love them "like brother and sister." The couple had left two school-age children behind in the care of Irma's sister. When their American hosts expressed amazement, their attitude was, "We want to live in a place without war and this is what we have to do."

The night before their Canadian hearing, a party was held for Irma and Antonio by the host family. A guest brought several records; one of them included "Cancion Infantil." Antonio unexpectedly ran from the room in tears. Irma explained that piece of music was one Antonio had sung regularly to their children in El Salvador.

All of the parents plan to find a way to bring their children "home" to them when they get settled. But I can remember how wistful Lillian became the night before her Canadian hearing, thinking about moving still further away from her homeland, "Sometimes, I feel like losing my country, my people, is losing my own family," she said. "Sometimes, I think if I went back, I could help, but then, I say, 'No, it is not possible.'" The only time she will go back, she tells me, is to retrieve her little girl.

So it is with great delight I open my paper to read of the Alvarenga family. They have so much ahead of them. She is just 16; he is 26. They have a baby, a new life together in a new land. They are filled with hope for the future. You can see it in their faces.

That's how I would like our new Central American friends to look. But for all their gratitude about moving to the comparative safety of Canada, there was pain in their eyes. They were missing family.

I can't believe how well we got to know them in so short a time, but sharing food and shelter, and throwing around a soccer ball will do that.

We especially found out how much they love their children. Enough to leave them behind. Incredible! I hope I never have to love mine...that much.

Spanish translator: Carol Alt

Viewpoints 1987

7

A Life Worth Living

"Be yourself. Everyone else is taken."
Oscar Wilde

Sitting directly behind the minister's wife in church one Sunday, my teenage-self decided that I would never want to be in her shoes. Literally. From head to toe, she looked dowdy in her black coat paired with an outdated navy blue hat, along with clunky shoes. Her demeanor seemed sad to me when I greeted her that morning. As I smoothed the skirt of my lime-green suit and adjusted my matching chapeau, my resolve strengthened. Being a minister's wife was not in my future. It didn't look like that much fun.

And so, 10 years later, I married a minister. During that decade I finished college, attended seminary, and worked in campus ministry for five years. I discovered that I loved being active in a church, participating in all its aspects and hanging with its people. When I met seminarian Mike and sparks flew, the commitment of helping a minister fulfill his calling was appealing. Challenging, yes, but interesting, a life very much worth living.

My husband's first parish was in a town of 225 in northern Illinois, smack in the middle of a cornfield—this, after living in New York, San Francisco, and

9

Chicago. The church supported itself on the public dinners it held throughout the year and everyone in the church was expected to prepare for them—including the minister's wife. I showed up in the church kitchen the morning of that first dinner shaking with fear. How long will it take them to find out what an absolute failure I was amidst pots and pans?

Not long, it turns out. I was expected to cut up a chicken. Cut. Up. A. Chicken. Didn't their parts come wrapped up in white butcher paper handed to you by a smiling man in a blood-stained apron?

I chopped, banged, and pulled, and tried to sneak glances to see how other women were doing it. Somehow, they were always able to find that little space between the breast and thigh where the knife slid between the two and produced a clean cut.

My battered half-a-chicken was finally, blessedly, rescued by a young farm wife who, sensing my panic, quietly reached across the counter and slid my poultry onto her own cutting board. Continuing to converse with her neighbors while she severed it perfectly, a sigh of relief escaped my lips. I left my post at the chopping block, seeking out the simplicity of tearing apart lettuce leaves. Now that I could do!

I saw graciousness in action that morning and grieved deeply when that farm wife unexpectedly died of cancer the next year, leaving behind a small daughter.

But that is the yin and yang of being a clergy wife— celebrating with someone one week at a joyous wedding, crying with them months later over a family tragedy. The job of being a minister's wife is being a part of our parishioners' lives in such an intimate way. Years later, when we reunite with those former congregants for an anniversary, we are still family. That feeling of closeness never goes away.

Twenty-eight years ago, our ministry brought us to Western New York. I joined a ministers' wives support group called RACHELS. We commemorate that brave woman of the Hebrew Scriptures who hid household gods under a camel's seat cushion as her family stole away to begin a new life.

We meet monthly, priding ourselves on having no officers, no dues and no agenda. Instead, we talk and listen and laugh a lot. We've become quite good at the listening part, fielding tales of family members dealing with dementia, children going astray, as well as conflicts between clergy and parishioners in our various churches. But then again, we have shared stories of joyous remarriages, new career paths and personal triumphs.

It's been an interesting journey. And as for stepping into a minister's wife's shoes? They seem to have fit pretty well. Admittedly, too big sometimes, a little pinched at others, but they started me on a journey I was blessed to be able to follow.

Women's Voices
1999

Home Closes, Crumbling Family

"I am not going to die. I'm going home
like a shooting star."
Sojourner Truth

My 93-year-old friend, Nora, passed away because she was told she had to move out of the assisted living facility she had lived in for 10 years.

"I wanted to die here," she said with tears in her eyes. Then she stopped eating and no amount of hand-feeding would part those lips. Two days after she moved into another facility, Nora quietly passed away.

Perhaps the staff in the new place thought her death so soon was happenstance. The staff in the old place knew better. She was, after all, our Nora. We knew her best. We loved her.

I was a staff member at United Church Home in North Buffalo, which closed last year after being in operation for 126 years. Eighty residents were relocated. Their average age was 87 and they were funny and smart, feisty and sweet-tempered. Many had not married nor had children. Family members had passed on and their friends were unable to visit. The staff turned out to be the ones who celebrated their birthdays and brought them goodies from the market.

We were family and it was a shock when the word went out that the place was closing. In recent years, we were faced with much competition—state-of-the-art facilities with shiny delicatessens and large, elegant lobbies. We had charm. But to the consumers, "stately" didn't cut it anymore.

But what really did us in was our shortfall. In 2002, it was more than $300,000. How could a non-profit facility ever make up such a sum? Forty percent of the residents received Supplementary Security Income; the rest paid with private funds. The SSI resident was not able to pay the full daily rate, so New York State reimbursed the facility $27 a day, but the room cost more than twice that amount. It was 2003 and New York State had not raised that subsidy since 1988.

In spite of that, in all those years, no resident was asked to leave because they were not able to pay their full share. We banded together with our sister facilities, protested our way to Albany for higher SSI subsidies and wrote letters to our legislators. The home instituted new programs, replaced an expensive food service and refrained from buying that much-needed van. Nothing worked.

We had a system in place to find new homes and the resident exodus went swiftly at first but slowed as the months rolled by—many assisted living facilities no longer admitted SSI recipients. The macabre joke among staff was that if any residents were left on closing day, we'd have to take one home with us. We were only half-kidding—the caring never stopped even as the census dwindled.

So the residents were dispersed and the staff was, too. But we were not alone—more than 55 adult care facilities in New York State closed their doors between 1995 and 2003.

We were caring, experienced health professionals who did the best we could in a financially strapped industry. We felt helpless as we watched seniors—our seniors— undergo the trauma of moving. At a time when they just wanted to live out their lives in a familiar environment, they suddenly had to face a new challenge.

Let's face it. Adjusting to a new home takes all of one's energy and energy is wanting in a 93-year-old. Nora wanted to die at our house. That has got to be the ultimate compliment.

October 2004

Something O.O. Would Do

*"Life is really simple but we insist
on making it complicated."*
Confucius

Every so often, while sitting in my car waiting for a light to change on Niagara Falls Boulevard, I read a bumper sticker on the car ahead, "If you can read this, thank a teacher." That would be my dad.

When I turned three, he sat me on his lap and read me the Sunday comics. Soon he was tracing the words with his finger and before long, I began recognizing a word or two. Eventually, there were two voices regaling over the size of Dagwood's monstrous sandwiches and the adventures of Popeye and his girlfriend Olive Oyl. With a brother named "Castor Oyl," how could I not love her? Her high energy ruled. She was always the damsel in distress.

I grew up thinking that reading was great fun and realized that the time spent with my dad would have been the envy of many Little Orphan Annies. So, at 11, when it came time to bake my first cake, I dedicated my unfolding interest in the culinary arts to him.

It was chocolate. Not that my father particularly liked chocolate, but I did. It was a from-scratch cake made by blending wet and dry ingredients along with melted chocolate. It came out of the oven with a delicious smell. The masterpiece was finished off with a lustrous black frosting, swirled back and forth with a butter knife making deep wavy lines.

It was also heavy. As I carried it from the kitchen to the dining table—we ate every meal in the dining room—it was hefty. I set it down dramatically in the middle of the table. "There," I said triumphantly, "and I want Daddy to have the first piece."

He blushed. It was the Irish half of him, the part that family and friends referred to when they said, "Roy has the map of Ireland on his face."

He took the knife offered him and carefully cut through the layers. Then he sliced a generous piece and slid it onto his dessert plate. With sober concentration—he realized the solemnity of the occasion—he took a bite.

His face, at first filled with anticipation, suddenly tightened and in two seconds he was out of his chair and gagging over the kitchen sink. The three of us still at the table looked at each other with stunned expressions. We heard him rinsing out his mouth, once, twice, three times. When he finally returned to his chair, while carefully averting my eyes, he declared, "Um, well, it's—different."

My older brother seated across the table had that all-knowing gleam in his eye I was so familiar with. "Did you put enough sugar in it?" he asked me.

"Yes, I did," I answered with attitude. "I followed all the directions."

"What does the sugar look like?" he pressed on.

"You know, the tall blue can with the spout."

"And the little girl with the umbrella?" he asked.

"Sure," I answered with conviction, giving him my best mean look.

"That was the salt," he declared triumphantly. "You put salt in instead of the sugar!"

This time, I blushed.

My dad raised his eyes from the table and caught mine. "Sounds like something Olive Oyl would do," he said with a wink. We both grinned.

For years afterward when he wanted to tease me about something I'd messed up, it was, ""Uh, oh, O.O. must have done that."

My first cake went right into the trash, adding several pounds to the garbage man's haul. What irony. The gift to my reading teacher was a disaster because I didn't read the blue can carefully enough.

February 2005

Every House Has a Heart

*"I have always drawn strength
from being close to home."*
Arthur Ashe

Houses have hearts. Some of them have ghosts, but all of them have hearts.

At night in the quiet, you can hear them beating. There's the refrigerator hum and furnace click and the wind blowing the pine tree against the siding. But the loudest beat comes when the previous owner comes back to visit.

Several summers ago there was a knock on our door. "I used to live here," the woman blurted out. "We were the first owners."

I invited her in to look around. Her voice ratcheted up with each new discovery.

"That's the fireplace my father put in and he took the wall down here, and oh, you've changed the kitchen."

She made her way to our window to gaze out into the backyard. "That's my grandfather's willow tree," she said, somewhat wistfully.

Really?

"Yes, he lived in New Jersey and brought a twig up and stuck it in the ground. Look at it, it must be 20 feet tall."

"Fifty," I say.

My daughter took a similar trip down memory lane. One day she dropped by our old hometown in Painesville, Ohio and visited the house we used to live in. Fifteen years had gone by and the colonial was on its second owner. Nevertheless, the current resident invited my daughter in immediately. Christa was thrilled.

After years of redecoration, the rooms looked very different. But my daughter was really itching to see her old bedroom and especially the closet. When she was about 10, with her dad in charge for the day, Christa and her neighborhood friends decided to paint the inside of her step-in closet.

With my husband's permission, they set to work with leftover paint and brushes scrounged from the basement. At day's end, the off-white walls boasted big blue hearts and red names in fancy letters, like "Christa" and "Cherise" and "Mark" along with giant tic-tac-toe boards and colored balloons and the Gilligan Island theme song.

All those years later, Christa climbed the stairs to the second floor and peeked into the pink-drenched room, still a little girl's abode. The wallpaper was different, the carpeting changed. Then Christa asked about the closet. The new owner opened its door with a flourish. It was exactly the same. The children's names were still there, the balloons, the hearts and the song.

"Somehow, we knew this meant something to the little girl who lived here, and we couldn't paint over it," the owner explained. "We had even decided because of the size of the name and the fanciness, it must have been Christa's room." They laughed together about a young girl's exuberance. Christa soon found herself overcome with nostalgia as her eyes filled with tears.

The visitor I had to my door didn't get to see our upstairs. She begged to see it, actually, to see how it had changed over the years. "It simply isn't presentable," I explained. I can still remember her disappointment. Perhaps she yearned to see a closet she had painted or initials she had carved into a windowsill.

Our kids are grown and I'm ready for unexpected guests now. Especially ones that remind me that a house, my house, has a heart that beats with the memories of the ones who have loved her.

I know I have the visitor's phone number somewhere. A return visit will get her the full attic-to-basement tour. Absolutely.

June 2005

Furnace Guy

"We cannot learn without pain."
Aristotle

It's the experts' fault, absolutely. Anything that has happened to us in the last few weeks is definitely their fault.

After a routine yearly check of our furnace, the first expert used his handy-dandy camera to take pictures of the inside, showed my husband four cracks in the heat exchanger and slapped a seal on the furnace. This, as we launched into a Buffalo winter. "You can't use it," he said. "If I let you use it, I could be arrested. Who knows when carbon monoxide will start oozing through those cracks?"

We checked the carbon monoxide monitor in the basement. It was not beeping, flashing red, nada. The poison gas had evidently not seeped through yet.

We listened to him. How could a minister and a writer refute the furnace guy? We called in the company that had originally installed the furnace, five years ago. Did you hear that? Five years ago! That furnace is just out of preschool, not even an adolescent yet. We still had a warranty on it, for goodness' sake.

They had to order special parts and would have them sent to us. It would be awhile. The cold started to settle in, somewhere around our ankles. We brought our space heater up from the basement. That didn't seem to help our comfort level so we borrowed a second. It got colder as ill winds seemed to pour through every crack of our 1950s house. We bought another heater. We put fires in the fireplace. We bought still another heater. We were now up to four. But it didn't seem to matter how many we had, we still huddled around our small kitchen table and sipped hot drinks. That is, until the circuit overloaded from the extra electricity, the lights went off, and one of us rushed down the basement stairs to switch the circuit breaker.

And then, when all the boards in the house were thoroughly frozen, 60-mile an hour winds came, knocked down backyard trees and our electricity went out. Now, of course, it didn't matter how many BTUs of portable heat we had. Nothing worked at this point. We lit candles throughout the house. The stone fireplace mantel was now so hot, the candles we set on top promptly melted.

We briefly considered going out to sit in our warmed-up car. Could we read the newspaper by the dome light? Finally, though, it was the mall that beckoned and we made excuses to escape into its heat and light.

"Don't we have to get Aunt Millie a birthday present?"

"That isn't until February."

"Let's do it today. We'll get a head start."

UPS finally delivered the special part and the original furnace company sent two employees to put it in. After they did, they agreed, "There were no cracks in that heat exchanger. The old one we just took out looked as good as the new one we put in."

We got on the phone to the "new" furnace guy. He came right over and tried to convince us that the small bump on the original exchanger, sitting in our driveway at this point, was a crack. Four? He didn't remember saying four cracks, only the one he was showing us.

We relied on the experts—all of them. They certainly knew what they were doing.

One hour after the last expert left, UPS rang our doorbell. They left another heat exchanger on our side porch. Another one, is that like a spare, just in case? Maybe we should save this one for the next routine inspection. You never know when a heat exchanger will come in handy. Will this story ever end?

After the season we've had, what's next? Locusts?

January 2006

Chautauqua Magic

"The most American spot in America…"
Teddy Roosevelt

"What's the Chautauqua Institution like?" asks the uninitiated. To those of us who visit the summer resort near Jamestown, N.Y. regularly, the question strikes us speechless but with a knowing smile. It's like we have a secret our sister has just told us but cannot reveal because we promised not to. But it's a special one, full of promise. Our eyes sparkle.

We will say that the program at the Institution encompasses the arts, religion, education, and recreation—something for everyone and then some. But describe it? Impossible. It has a milieu, an atmosphere. Touting civil discourse, it embodies civility. People gift others with their talents or thoughtfulness or unexpected problem-solving. Instead, we say with meek resignation, as we've said a hundred times before, "You have to be there to experience it."

I just returned from a season at the Chautauqua Institution writing for the Daily Chautauquan newspaper. This was my third, and each summer my belief in its magic ratchets up some more.

Anecdote 1: The Hall of Philosophy is one of the venues for the lectures featured at the Institution.

Modeled after a columned, open-sided Greek structure, when the seats under the roof are filled, the overflow listeners find themselves standing under an open sky. One afternoon, while listening to a Pulitzer Prize winner, I found myself on the outside looking in. It began to rain, hard. Not dressed for it, my heart sank. A once-in-a-lifetime event, I had cleared my calendar for weeks to hear this lecture. I huddled closer under the overhang but I could not escape the water as it cascaded down the back of my neck; I would have to leave. Suddenly, out of the seated audience, a woman strode over to me, opened her umbrella and handed it to me. Startled, I reached for it and stayed for the entire talk. As the lecture ended, she retrieved it and with a quick smile, was gone. I will most likely forget the words of the dignitary but remember a stranger's kindness. A Chautauquan moment...

Anecdote 2: Parents and their two-year-old twin daughters boarded the free but crowded bus that tootles around the grounds. Everyone was finally seated and all was quiet until the bus began to move. Sydney began to cry—loudly protesting something, but no one knew quite what. The parents sat perplexed. Suddenly, the bus driver started to sing with gusto, "The wheels on the bus go round and round, round and round, round and round. The wheels on the bus go round and round all around Chautauqua." One by one passengers joined in, "The wheels on the bus..." Sydney soon stopped crying and with a smile on her face and along with sister Madison, joined in the chorus. It takes a village...

Anecdote 3: Ken Anderson from Bath, N.Y. was enjoying his dinner in the Hurlbut Church dining room, filled with Chautauquans sitting at long tables. After he introduced himself to those around him, a tablemate remarked, "With that low voice, I bet you can sing 'Old Man River'". Anderson, a bass who actually specializes in performing Paul Robeson concerts, paused for a moment before sliding into song: "Old Man River, that Old Man River..." At the end of his rendition, the entire dining room burst into applause. "What do you do when a 92-year-old man asks you to sing?" Anderson said later. "You sing. I sing in a heartbeat anyway," he admitted, "if anybody asks me to."

This is just a small sampling of memorable Chautauqua moments taking place throughout the nine-week season. But you know? It's like I said when we started this conversation: "You really have to be there."

October 2006

There is Only One, but,
Oh, What a One!

"If nothing is going well, call your Grandmother."
Italian Proverb

In the 1970s when my husband and I began to expand our family, our closest friends and we followed the Zero Population Growth dictum: you had only enough babies to replace yourself. We were convinced that it was the most efficient way to avoid overpopulation and therefore, following that route was essential for the health of the ecosphere.

We were not very sophisticated in those days: "Carbon footprint?" What was that? We did know that having a third child would use up more food, water, fossil fuels, and trees along with producing more rubbish and pollution, adding to the myriad problems of too many people and all their stuff. That was the hey-day of plastics, after all (remember "The Graduate"?) and where would all those plastics go but into landfill after landfill. Not on our watch, if we could help it.

Besides, didn't we mothers have just two hands, one each to guide those babies across the street and through life? God must have been telling us something.

This was also the era when motherhood was beginning later. Most of us started our marital journeys in apartments, not mini-mansions like the present generation. It took time for us to get settled. We were in our 30s by the time the first house came, and thereafter came the children. We did things in order: marriage, house, and babies—two and a half-years apart, OF COURSE.

We had a lot of thinking to do before the decision of just two and a lot of explaining to our extended family. My mother couldn't understand our reasoning: she had often apologized for not providing me with more siblings. One of five children, she always thought big families were the way to go. She married a man with seven brothers and sisters, after all. But there were just my brother and I, and years later, my husband and I perpetuated that number.

Now that we are in our mature years, I look around and see a scarcity of that most magical of commodities— grandchildren. My neighbor, for instance, has four married children and just two grandchildren. Relatives have none or only one. Two kids seem unwieldy. Three seems like a tribe. Four? Forgetaboutit.

Recently, we attended our granddaughter's gymnastic class to see what they had learned in their weeks of classes. There were nine adorable four and five-year-old girls, dressed in footless leotards or thigh-length tights, pony-tails swinging. They pencil-rolled and balanced-beamed and tunnel-crawled up a storm. They were all harum-scarum arms and legs much of the time, but the parents and grands and brothers and sisters appreciated it all and applauded like crazy.

At the end of the session, the teacher, kneeling down in front of each, stamped the back of their hands. The stamp on my granddaughter's said "terrific" and I read it out loud as we walked down the hallway of the school to the exit door. She looked up at me with her big blue eyes and asked, "Grandma, was I terrific?" "Oh, my, yes," I said, squeezing that hand, "Super terrific."

It might be that this little charmer will be the only one we are blessed with. That is just fine with me. There may be only one, but oh, what a one....

July 2008

New Life Fills Church

"Any God I ever felt in church I brought in with me."
Alice Walker

As a part of a dozen or so parishioners remaining in St. John's United Church of Christ, a struggling South Buffalo, N.Y. church, it was painful to hear the protests when we began talking about closing its doors forever. We just didn't have the finances or even the will to keep it another season. It was difficult for my husband, who had been pastoring there for several years, and me, to listen to the sorrow in their voices.

"But I was baptized in this church," one parishioner exclaimed.

"My children grew up here," another said with tears in her eyes.

"My parents donated that stained glass window," remembered the organist.

The cornerstone on the small white church said "1901". Founded by Germans who settled in the area, anecdotes hint that kegs of beer were distributed to volunteer builders as an incentive to keep them working. An unobtrusive building, it was tucked back among modest houses. When we came out of services on warm

Sunday mornings, neighbors smiled at us as they waved from porch chairs across the street.

The building showed wear and tear. The front door cracked, the window boxes sat forlorn and empty. During a fierce winter storm, the stately tree in the front yard came crashing down, and there it lay for a couple of years until Buffalo street workers finally toted it away.

Inside, the building declined as well. The kitchen, not being used, seemed to rust in place. Wind blew through the caulking in the sanctuary windows.

There was the shared worry that if we put it on the market no one would claim the place that meant so much to us for so long. We had visions of the building, standing alone and empty with rain and snow finding its way through roof fissures.

Time came when the faithful few who showed up each Sunday had to make a decision, because, as a wise elder noted, "We cannot afford the high heating bills one more winter." Heads nodded. There would be a sale.

To give us time to get used to the idea, we tackled the chore of cleaning out church closets. Every week after service, another box was resurrected and its wonders unfolded. One held the communion set, another, altar cloths that were changed according to the liturgical season. What to do with them? Donated? Given away? Thrown away? Everything found a home—somewhere.

Tucked in one of the last containers was the beloved Christmas nativity set. Seeing it brought back the memories of Christmas Eves when the children of the church had the honor to place each ceramic figure in exactly the right spot.

There was an awkward pause. Who would get to enjoy this treasure under their own tree? Finally, one family carefully wrapped Mary, Joseph, and baby Jesus in tissue paper and took them home, while another carried the Wise Men and the shepherds to theirs.

Hardly had we told anyone about our decision when a house church in the Southtowns contacted us, asking to view the building. They were eager, they told us, to find a home for their growing congregation. In the simplest of real estate dealings, the newcomers took over.

Six months later, feeling nostalgic, my husband and I and several former parishioners scheduled a Sunday morning to attend a worship service at our old church on Lilac Street. Warmly welcomed, we accepted an offer to tour the facility. The changes were astonishing! The pews had been refinished and the floor sanded and polished to a high gloss. Although disappointed to see the stained-glass windows replaced, the sanctuary glistened as sunlight poured through the clear glass. Renovations throughout the building showed the loving care of master carpentry.

During the service, with no musical accompaniment, the church members' voices mirrored a harmony-filled a cappella choir at its very best. Listening to the heavenly sounds soar, our hearts filled with joy that our little building was once again a vibrant and sacred space blessed by God.

February 2009

Loving the Job

"When you are asked to do a job, tell 'em, 'Certainly, I can!' Then get busy and find out how to do it."
Theodore Roosevelt

My husband retired while I was still working at my fulltime job. We slid into a nice rhythm of his shopping for the groceries and making a delicious dinner every night for me to come home to.

It was not an unusual situation. Sitting around the lunch table at work, out of the seven women gathered there, most were in the same situation: wife still working, spouse home stirring the stew. We all agreed that it was not what we had foreseen but it was working out pretty well. A couple of the husbands even threw in a load of laundry once in a while.

Then that same secure job I had not given one moment of concern about, dissolved. The staff was sliced into shreds because of budgets not passed, grants denied, and those dreaded cutbacks. Suddenly, I was a statistic—one of those men and women pushing the number of unemployed soaring past even those of the Great Depression.

The first days of not setting the alarm were heady ones. There were so many projects we wanted to finally get around to. That lasted for, well, maybe two months or so. And then getting up in the mornings wasn't a very exciting prospect. Instead, the days began to seem endless.

"So what should we do today?" we'd ask each other, followed by a long pause while one of us tried to think of something more exciting than still another trip to the Farmers' Market. It was a grim reminder of actress Brooke Shields' comment citing the reason for her breakup with husband, tennis pro Andre Agassi. "We couldn't agree on how to spend the day."

My husband and I discussed the possibilities. Auditing college courses? Multiple visits to the library? Craft classes? None of them beckoned to us. As a minister of 33 years, my husband had helped people in a tangible way. He missed that, so after prayerful thought, he took a Visiting Nurses course to become certified as a health care aide. Working several hours a day with male clients, many cared for by Hospice, Mike sees his new profession as a continuation of his call to minister to the sick and elderly.

I, on the hand, missed a community of professionals to hang out with each day. Who was there to gossip with? (I love to gossip.) Or banter about world affairs? Or decide which costume to wear on Halloween?

Writing on my computer was fine for a couple of hours, but then I found myself heading for the TV around 11 a.m. to watch "The View," where four lively, funny women discussed hot topics. How come they had somewhere to go every day and I didn't? One day, during a commercial, I picked up the want-ad section of the paper and glanced at it. Then I began to read it every day. Maybe there really was something out there.

There was and there is. I found a part-time job I love— teaching children to read in a one-on-one situation for a learning center. I can't tell you what satisfaction I get from those sessions of exploding the code of the written word.

Planning for the couple of hours a day I work outside of the home gives a framework to the rest of the day's schedule. Phone calls get made, bills get paid and articles get written. Everything simply flows better.

And when my session with a pony-tailed seven-year-old is done and she calls out after me, "See you tomorrow, Miss Lois?" I can say with heartfelt feeling, "Absolutely--cannot wait!"

October 2009

Just a Kid

Stress is caused by not camping enough.
Pinterest

I'm just a kid who likes to go to camp. OK, so I'm a Senior Kid.

What do I like about it? The eating with a bunch of other people, not just our small family. The cooking someone else does. The singing, loud and off-key that I'm encouraged to do. The comfortable clothes I'm allowed to schlep around in. The huge swimming pool I don't have in my own backyard. It's a trip.

And a short one, at that. The conference center in Dunkirk we attend logs just one hour and 10 minutes from our Tonawanda driveway to its peaceful haven on Lake Erie.

Our family has been going to Dunkirk Camp and Conference Center for 27 years, with the third generation beginning to enjoy the fruits of labor. Thousands of volunteers have contributed to its growth and upkeep for 88 years, many of them providing brawn as well as brains. They dug holes for the pool, sided the cabins, painted the dining hall, led Bible study and called out square dances. It's a joy to be part of the community who "enters to learn and departs to serve".

I've learned through the years that no matter the circumstances, good memories are made. One year, as a counselor, my cabin of six 10-year-olds were bored out of their minds when all it did was rain for days. That wet stuff pelted us from morning to night and we sloshed through the mud in boots all over the grounds.

Ah, yes, the mud. Ankle deep toward the end of the week when the rain finally stopped, the kids were desolate. Even though it stopped raining, playing tetherball was out and the pool session was cancelled along with the camp-wide softball game. However, our enterprising campers rose to the occasion. They shed their boots and created a mud slide. Stopping short of getting their clothes dirty—let's face it, they had very few clean ones left—they slid as far as they could without falling down into the slime.

The counselors, caught up in the spirit of turning lemons into lemonade, hatched a variation on the activity idea. "OK," we conceded, "go get your bathing suits on and have a ball." The campers were ecstatic about the idea and ended up having a wonderful afternoon.

Years later, when I meet any of these mud-sliders, I ask, do they remember the good food, the inspiring studies and the trips to the Lake Erie beach? No, they don't. Instead, they remember best the great fun they had on a mudslide made out of God's incessant waterfall and a pile of dirt.

I remember best the work weekends at the camp, the time in spring when 80 or so people get together to open the camp for the summer youth and family camps. During the day, everyone works hard scraping, sanding, painting, sweeping, mopping, and polishing. Then, on Saturday night, all put aside their work tools to join in a Hoe-Down. Generations of families take to the floor of the dining room to bounce to the strains of a live band playing the Virginia Reel and the Mexican Hat Dance. Who wouldn't enjoy the sight of a five-year-old charmer with a smile on her face and a wiggle in her hips doing the Hokey Pokey?

We play just as hard as we work at camp.

It's almost time to make the trek from Tonawanda to Dunkirk again. The whole family can't wait to work and play and build those memories. Maybe, just maybe, if we're lucky, it will rain....

May 2010

Take Two Doctors and Call Me in the Morning

"Never go to a doctor where office plants have died."
Erma Bombeck

Ooooh, those doctors! There's so many of them! It's enough to give me a pain in my sacroiliac.

Years ago you had one doctor for a lifetime, the relationship shortened by either his death or yours. He (almost always a man) remembered when you had the measles and knew where the chickenpox marks were. He knew your eccentricities; you knew his.

Knowing you gag at the sight of needles, he coaxed you to look over his shoulder and concentrate on that Norman Rockwell on the wall. When you resisted taking still another pill, he reassured you that you could try it out, come back in two weeks and "we will talk about it again."

The generation before us had only one doctor, after all, and they had survived, and survived well. My mother was 96 and still talking about her favorite doctor, Dr. Linsky, in years past. He saw her through two tough deliveries, numerous anxiety attacks, and still called her playfully, "Princess," whenever he saw her. Those visits to his office were in themselves therapeutic. She loved the attention from an old friend.

These days, no one doctor knows all about you. Your primary doctor sees you once a year for your physical, takes your blood pressure, peers into ears and throat, listens to your heart, and pokes your belly. She barely glances at you as she types your report into a laptop.

Then she refers you to the physicians mining more specialized fields. Acid reflux problems? "Here is the name of a gastroenterologist."

Sugar slightly high? "I'm sending you to an endocrinologist."

Fatigue? "Let's see what a stress test says. Here's the name of a cardiologist."

My primary physician was so into referrals that a doctor she referred me to for an endoscopy threw me out the door! When I told him my symptoms of digestive distress, he seemed annoyed. "Why did your doctor send you here?" he demanded. "Maybe I do a scope and it turns out to be sinus drainage." We both agreed I would come back another day if a dinner of pork and sauerkraut had its way with me.

In the meantime, the doctors were actually cancelling out each other's prescriptions. The cardiologist told me to stop taking my daily dose of folic acid. The endocrinologist advised me to cancel the monthly B12 shots.

"Not needed," they both said. Now how does that make the primary doctor feel who prescribed both? I don't even want to know.

Who's on first here? Certainly not me.

Take the example of one specialist I see when I have flare-ups. Although my record has been updated, he bursts into the exam room asking the same questions but perhaps not the right ones, like what diseases my body has invented since last we met. "Doctor, you know I now have diabetes," I tell him.

"Oh, really? Well, now, this medication I'm giving you," he says with aplomb, "will raise your sugar." And out the door he goes with a flourish. Now, how do I deal with that information? I guess that's my call.

Referrals are good for one year, but who remembers when that begins or ends? I see one of my specialists every four months, another yearly, still another every two. Am I still on the good side of a referral or have I expired? It gets confusing.

And who to call to request one? The endocrinologist works most closely with the throat and neck physician. Should I call him? On the other hand, my primary physician originally directed me to the throat and neck guy. Maybe she's the one to contact.

It's a conundrum I feel clear through to my sacroiliac.... Could this mean another specialist???

September 2010

Voting is What We Do

"I vote for my daughter and for her future."
Christa Vidaver

The first time I went into a voting booth (the ones with curtains—remember those?), I blew it. Clueless about the procedure, but unwilling to admit it, I pushed down the levers under the names familiar to me, and waited. What? No bells, no whistles, no flashing lights? Well, then, obviously my votes had not registered. So, I pushed the levers up again. That did it, I thought, flinging open the curtain. It didn't occur to me until much later that I had not-so-cleverly cancelled out my own vote.

The importance of this Constitutional right came home to me in a dramatic way while traveling on a European train. A man sat in the corner of our car while we American tourists chattered away. Suddenly, leaning toward us and with a heavy accent, he whispered, "Do you know how close we are to the Iron Curtain right now?" Fear spread across his face and showed in his body language—drawn shoulders, pinched face. He then leaned back and stared out the window into the abyss of a dark night, saying not another word. His anxiety pouring across the aisle, I sat frozen in my seat, realizing for the first time, how fearful it must be to live forever under the rule of a dictator.

I think of that man around election time and how lucky we are to live in a free country where we have the privilege to vote. "If you live in this house, you vote!" is a mantra my kids grew up with. Our son and daughter vote faithfully and the political conversations around our kitchen table are lively and thought-provoking.

One year the Primary campaign in our town was especially fun. We had a local candidate full of energy, who phoned us personally four times and came to our door four more. We live on the busiest street in town, but as his father trolled their car along the multiple-lane road, the candidate jumped in and out, running across lawns, knocking on doors and leaving pamphlets. His enthusiasm became a family joke, but it added so much to the election, it felt like we should invite him over for a late summer barbeque.

I've come a long way from that college student who didn't know how the voting machine worked. This fall, I attended a training seminar for election inspectors put on by the Erie County Board of Elections and learned a lot about the new system, like how to scan the ballots into a machine that looks disturbingly like the town totes we slide our garbage into!

The class was led by men with decades of experience who shared with us the possibilities of a day that begins at the polls at (yawn!) 5:30 a.m. and lasts about 16 hours. Along the way, we learned how to ensure privacy for every voter, how to operate a ballot-marking device for a person with disabilities and what to do when the polls close at nine and there is still a line out the door. Oh, and most of all, what flavor doughnuts to have on hand when an election board staff member meanders by.

I can tell from the chain letters some of my email friends send that they are not on the same side of the political fence that I am. But that is so not important. I wish every one of them the sunniest day possible on Election Day so they too will vote. Because voting is the most important thing we do in this democracy.

Realizing our kids, Mark and Christa, see it as part of their birthright? That gets my vote every time.

November 2010

Wind and the Willow

Fall down seven times, get up eight.
Japanese Proverb

Never mind that our garage tilted like the Tower of Pisa, looking like something had smacked it hard on the left and forever forced it to bend to the right. Visitors walking on the driveway toward it stared in awe. "Does that garage actually lean?" they asked incredulously. Living with its deformity for 25 years, we treated it like a beloved but embarrassing relative. "Yes, it does," we would answer, "but somehow it does the job."

One very windy spring day last year knocked the stuffing out of the 50-foot willow tree in our backyard. Coming down with a roar, it sheared off much of that garage and a corner of the house.

I had a good view of the calamity. Sitting in my second-story office, I glanced out the window to watch the willow hurtling straight at me. With a terrified scream, I ran out the door and down the stairs. The next day, the family gathered for Mother's Day worship service in the church sanctuary giving thanks that everyone was safe after such a harrowing experience.

Once the shock wore off, we realized how much we actually had lost. We never did have the opportunity to enjoy one last picnic in our backyard under the shade of that tree. A good part of our brand-new roof, summer patio, slate walkway, and perennial garden (Will the beautiful lavender clematis ever come back?) was lost, along with everything inside the garage. A limb catapulting from the tree tore right through its roof, knocking the door off the track and making it inoperable. Our stuff was as much entombed as a mummy in a sarcophagus.

The garbage tote, along with the recycling bin, were sealed in. What to do with the garbage? We produce a lot—we've often marveled at how much we three can accumulate in a week. We'd just have to borrow a portion of one of our neighbor's totes. But which one? Certainly not the large family whose refuse was already overflowing each week. Whom to ask? We finally settled on a dear retired couple down our street who seemed glad to stuff our plastic bags in beside theirs. Being caring neighbors, they came to visit our backyard and commiserate with us about the damage.

What do we do about the lawnmower that is locked inside as well? "A borrower nor a lender be," but it was summer. Obviously, we had to keep up neighborhood appearances and not let the grass grow tall. Who can forget the Kenmore resident who cultivated a wildflower garden and enraged the natives? It's noted that he doesn't live in Kenmore anymore. After a family caucus, we made the decision to choose the most agreeable relative in the family and ask to borrow his mower. Again and again.

The rebuilding seemed to take forever, almost five months. To celebrate its completion, we held a Labor

Day party (very appropriate—lots of labor went into the new digs). We invited friends over to view our newly-minted cedar shakes and raw-wood picket fence. Draping the patio columns in reams of blue and red crepe paper, as the excitement built, my husband and I dramatically sliced the festive wrappings with a pair of scissors while the guests cheered.

We noticed it sometime after the shock of the event wore off. Coming up the driveway, I stopped and looked, then looked again. The garage doesn't lean anymore. The willow tree set it straight. With a whoosh and a swipe, it knocked that garage on the side of the head, and said, "Stand up there, my man, and look proud." And we will be forever grateful.

April 2011

The Story of My Coat

"Didn't your Mom tell you to hang up your coat?"
Lois Vidaver

With fall here and winter coming, here's the dilemma: Where do we put our coats? For those of us who like a meal out, that is a very timely question.

Last year I was disappointed to discover that when our favorite breakfast restaurant altered its space, they remodeled the coat rack out of existence. Eating there once a month with a group of friends, we used that rack so much that we often brought in our own hangers to make up for a shortage. It also had a shelf above for our hats and scarves, which, when the winter winds blow, many of us wear. We live and work, after all, in Buffalo. You know, the land of the arctic breezes, where snow flies in the air and ice forms underfoot and people actually wear COATS???

One day, after the remodeling, when four of us were comfortably seated in one of their booths, I realized that there was no room left for my outer jacket. I waved a server down. "Where can I put my coat?" I asked. He began looking for an alternative.

"Put it on the chair across from me," the man sitting at the next table suggested. "It will make me feel like my Mary is sitting there," he added, wistfully. The server, relieved, complied and I thanked the man for his thoughtfulness. I said a silent prayer for him and his missing companion.

Speaking to the manager later, we pointed out the spot where the coat rack used to be. In that spot now is a picture. Could he not replace it with the rack? Well, no, said he, "corporate" insisted on the new decor.

The next restaurant we went to also did not have a place for coats. After we were seated in our for-two-only booth (a cozy size), I realized the only place for my coat to fit might be under the seat on the floor. I looked under the seat. No space. Again, I called over the server, "Where can I put my coat?" I asked. He transferred it to a four-seater. We were crammed into a two-seater; my coat was sprawled comfortably in a four-seater. This did not add up, so we shoved my coat into a corner and joined it for a much more comfortable meal.

The last restaurant experience was breakfast (of course!) in a pancake house. They, too, have remodeled (restaurants, let's face it, do very well in WNY) and again, the coat rack, the roomiest one we have ever encountered, had disappeared. The manager explained that it made way for a mural depicting the farmstead of the restaurant's founder. Is the artwork of rolling farmlands really more important than the comfort of its customers? This place has installed hooks on the end of the booths. Perhaps they will work, perhaps not. Somehow, they may prove inadequate for the long wool coat I wear for after-church brunches.

What to do? One solution is simply not to frequent these restaurants. But that's not possible because it's hard to find one that has coat closets anymore! Should we start signing petitions, because certainly other people are not wild about sitting in restaurants wearing their cold, clammy outer clothing, are they?

Maybe the answer is to get a bigger booth or table than we need just to pile on our coats, scarves, and hats. Yes, that is the solution, now that I think about it. When the server asks, "How many?" I will say, "There are four people and four coats but the coats can double up. Six seats, please."

October 2013

64

Clearing of the Trees

"It looks like the apocalypse."
Brighton Road neighbor

Two neighbors stood with me, curbside on Brighton Road, midway between Fries Road and Niagara Falls Boulevard, while we studied the landscape. First looking to our left, then to our right, one finally said, "It seems eerie." The other nodded. "It looks like the apocalypse."

Within a period of several days, to mark the beginning of major road construction, the large maple trees standing guard on our curb lawns were shorn of their upper limbs. Nothing but naked trunks were left.

I thought briefly about contacting a chainsaw sculptor to ask about the possibility of turning Brighton into an outdoor sculpture gallery. Offering homage to winged flocks of now-treeless birds, an innovative tree artist would portray a cardinal on one stump, a woodpecker or a dove on others. With a little imagination, our county road would become a Town of Tonawanda tourist attraction. Canadian shoppers cruising down our road heading to the Boulevard Mall would love it.

We moved to Brighton Road 30 years ago against the advice of a neighboring homeowner. "It's too dirty," she said. But we bought a house on the four-lane road anyway, simply because we liked it best.

Dirt is dirt and it never really bothered us. We hosed the car emission residue off the siding once a year and went through multiple rags to clean our car windows on misty mornings. They turned black. "It would be dirtier," I told my husband, "if it weren't for those big maples up and down the street."

We loved the trees for many reasons. They not only cleaned. They also cooled our houses, gave charm to the landscape and covered up the myriad of cables and tall poles on our side of the road.

Now though, the trees are completely gone, reduced to heaps of sawdust on the curbs. Those wires and poles ARE our view, and none too pretty.

But good things have come out of this lengthy (three-month) construction project. Because the usual Brighton traffic is intimidating, it cuts down on neighborly visits. Now that it's closed to all vehicles, it's given us a chance to cross over the great divide for the first time in years to chat about this new look.

Truth be told, with the thousands of cars buzzing by every day, living on Brighton is much more akin to living in the city than in the suburbs. There are noises of every kind coming from motorcycles, car radios, and emergency vehicles. But since the end of August, it is more like living in the country. It's very, very quiet, especially most nights, so different sounds are reaching our ears. With people traffic on the increase, we hear bikers calling out to each other, skateboarders whizzing by, dogs barking and the fireworks over Coca-Cola Field exploding on Friday nights.

We see more sky, too, reveling at the huge orange sun hanging low over Maple Road. Now that we can see it, we take the time to admire the care our neighbor across the street puts into his curb appeal. And, as we drive under a canopy of oak and maple and locust trees on our neighboring streets, we no longer take their beauty for granted.

We certainly admire the ingenuity of our neighbors. After the trunk of the tree on their curb lawn was felled, they sliced it into rustic-looking seats to be used on their family patio out back. Now that's taking a minus and turning it into a plus.

We Brighton folks are very resilient....

October 2014

Downsizing is My Game

Our yearly church rummage sale inspires me. For one thing, I am a de-clutterer and proud of it. Therefore, I'm glad to have an official excuse to go through my house, tossing out the unneeded and unwanted. One friend asked me recently if I was downsizing. "I've been downsizing for 50 years," said I, without exaggeration.

I think the realization that enough stuff is probably too much, happened when I was growing up in a household where my Dad was a civil engineer in charge of overseeing airport construction throughout the Northeast. His responsibilities took about a year each time and departure time to the next location always seemed rushed. I kept my bedroom drawers neat and tidy so when word came to move on, I was ready in minutes to throw my belongings into the nearest box and trek on to the next adventure.

Moving around stopped 30 years ago but I'm still culling out my belongings. When our rummage sale was announced, I dug deeper. Using the adage, "If you haven't used it in a year, toss," I took it at its word.

We had a special treat buried in a basement plastic bin: silver serving dishes from my husband's mother's family.

Mike had a great-aunt who had passed them down to our family. We had never used them (all that polishing!) and it was time to make the decision about their future. Although we had tried to sell them, dealers were not interested; they were silver-plated rather than all-silver. We decided to include them, too, in the rummage sale.

The event is well-organized. Each of the rooms off the main hallway of the church is dedicated to particular items: household, books and children's items. So the night before the sale, I set my treasures along with the others. The silver shone more elegantly than the household items that surrounded them—maybe that was a good thing. Surely, the large round serving plate with three feet supporting it, the candy dish, and the cookie tray would stand out to a discerning buyer. I could only hope.

The next day, I could not resist going to visit them. Did someone pick them up to give them a new home? After poking around in some of the other rooms, I entered the one marked "Household," then slowly made my way around the tables until I spotted my silver beauties. I realized they had an audience. With a jeweler's magnifying glass in one eye, a man held the silver tray in his hand while he read the writing on its back. The other two pieces were piled on top of one another nearby. I stood transfixed at his elbow; he paid me no mind. Should I interrupt his concentration to tell him the family story?

"Are you going to buy the silver?" I finally had to ask. "No," he said, never taking his eyes off the piece he was holding. "It's silver-plate."

"Yes, I know," I said. "My husband's great-aunt was a missionary in White Horse in the Yukon for 40 years and she was sure the Queen of England would come by to visit someday. She collected the silver serving plates so she would have them to serve with."

An hour later, after seeing the rest of the sale, I returned to the spot where the silver had been. Only one was left. The big tray and the candy dish were gone. Someone had indeed given them a new home. Perhaps the man with the eyepiece liked our family story.

I neglected to tell him the Queen never did show up.

January 2015

A Fishy Story

"The best way out is always through."
Robert Frost

I am trying to remember when we first started talking about moving.

It was about eight years ago when my husband had quintuple-bypass heart surgery. That began a number of conversations having to do with our home that we have loved for 33 years. But it has a laundry in the basement and too many stairs. After some real-estate research, I discovered spring was the best month to market.

Two years ago we became serious about the first step, de-cluttering. We cleaned out every drawer and every closet in the house, bringing bric-a-brac to charity shops in town. We offered stuff to our daughter, who first said, "It's beautiful, Mom, but not my style," then kept her grandmother's gold-rimmed china for holiday dinners after all.

It was a good feeling—lean and mean. We'd open a drawer and the three or four items in there would literally swim around. Until they didn't.

I don't know how it happened but the moving keeps getting put off, and the drawers started filling up again.

Right in the middle of that big downsizing craze, it was on our minds that our 50th anniversary was coming up the following September. Our event planner daughter said one night, "How about having the party in your backyard?"

We gulped and said, "What a great idea! We won't put the house up for sale this spring. We have a party to plan!" And so our son Mark and daughter Christa did, and it was incredible, could not have been nicer.

During that fall, county officials announced that our street, Brighton Road, would be torn up and not usable until December 1st. Perfect, we would put our house on the market in early spring 2015 and there would be a brand new road to brag about. We would do the painting and redecorating (that bathroom sink has got to go!) that winter.

Except we had more winter than ever. The one from hell. It blew and was freezing cold and all we really did was hunker down in front of the fireplace and try to survive. Energy we did not have. Our neighbor did, though. He sided his house. "It looks beautiful," we said to each other, "and will certainly help the value of ours."

That summer we enjoyed the backyard more than ever, knowing it would probably be the last year.

In the fall of 2015, we obviously needed some pushing, so we invited a real estate agent in. She went through, underscored what we had to do to get it ready to show and we signed up again for the push. Yes, we would scrape and paint and sand and refinish. We certainly would put the winter to good use. Except that we didn't.

Because this is the late winter season that Fishy died. Fishy is the prize my granddaughter won at Brighton Field Days eight years ago. He thrived and grew big and fat. One day he was swimming around in his fish water happy as a…well…lark. But then his tank got cleaned and new seascape ornaments introduced. The next day, he was found floating on his back. All that clean stuff he could not put up with.

"Fishy will be buried in Grandma's backyard," the Facebook post said. "Watch this space for further information." The plan is that when Mother Earth gives us permission to dig, we will landscape his burial site with flowering perennials so we will always know where Fishy is.

Sell the house this spring with the ground still soft from a family funeral? It just doesn't seem right. Maybe next year.

April 2016

Smiles Abound

"Don't cry because it's over,
smile because it happened."
Dr. Seuss

I had the best birthday celebration this year. Because it was a Big Zero one, our daughter Christa pulled off a surprise that completely delighted me. Our immediate family headed toward a private room in a restaurant but when we walked in, several friends had joined the party. After dinner, one of them brought forth a tray with eight votive candles on it. Each candle, she instructed me, represented a decade of my life and I was to share one remembrance from each.

What to tell? I reminded all those gathered that not only, in my advanced age, was my hearing going and my eyes failing but my memory was slipping too. I determined to pull myself together, however, and try not to make a complete fool of myself.

My granddaughter Isabella did the honors by lighting the first candle as I rapidly (as one could at my age) searched for an appropriate memory. "What happened to you between the age of 0 and 10?" someone gently prodded.

Well, let's see. My first memory of life was my father locking my mother out of the house at a late hour when I was about five. As she pounded on the front door, I crept downstairs, pulled a chair over, climbed up, and opened the lock to let her back in. He wouldn't, but I did.

No, I thought to myself, I couldn't rightly tell that one. I realized at that moment my memories had to go through a split-second selective process. Hmmm, talk about a challenge!

I settled on an exciting time when I was eight. My father, uncle and I, accompanied my brother to Penn Station where he would catch a train, arrive at Camp Lejeune, N.C. on his 18th birthday and begin his new life as a Marine. A World War II hero, he later earned a Bronze Star and Purple Heart at Iwo Jima. Pride welled up in me as I shared this story.

A memory from when I was 10 to 20-years-old-- another nudge, another candle was lit. It was the time I almost did not graduate from my New York City high school. Every senior had to jump into the pool and swim its length before they received their diploma. I remember (long after the deadline was passed) rounding up friends who would come and support me. Finally the minute arrived. The coach, standing on the side of the deep end egged me on, "You can do this, Lois!" My friends cheered as I and my terror took the plunge. Desperately flailing my arms and legs like a turbo engine, I made it to the first set of steps leading to the deck. I never did swim the length, but we all celebrated as if I had. I preened like a champion.

For my seventh decade, I talked about the shock of losing a job I loved when the facility closed unexpectedly. I had pictured myself retiring in that job and leaving with a celebrative lunch amid my colleagues. It was not to be. What to do? Within a short time, I filled the hours of my days with an opportunity that made me feel I had won the lottery, teaching reading to special needs children at a local learning center. I related the joy I felt when a young charge at the end of a session, reminded me with outstretched arms, "Hugs, Miss Lois."

If I could have done it again, I would have shared with that wonderful gathering the wisdom of Dr. Seuss, "Don't cry because it's over, smile because it happened."

November 2016

Holidays at the Movies

*"I took the bus to Santa Monica
when I was eight to see double features.
Movies touch my heart."*
Mike Vidaver

The Vidavers have a holiday tradition that has nothing to do with hanging mistletoe, sending out greeting cards or devouring Grandma's stuffing. It may not even be a very unusual custom these days, but at the time we started it, more than 40 years ago, it was.

We spend our holiday afternoons at the movies. The tradition started because my husband, a clergyman, generally has worship service obligations at our church. So, with our families hundreds of miles away, we were stay-at-homes.

On the day of the celebration, of course, we did the usual rituals, opening presents while fielding phone calls from around the country ("Merry Christmas! Wish we were closer!"). But after the hoopla, there were hours to go before two over-stimulated children would finally settle down and go to sleep. What to do?

The first time I remember us trekking to the nearest movie house was on a New Year's Day when the kids were six and eight. Having attended a midnight Watch Service at our church the night before, a nap sounded pretty good to the grownups. But our kids beat us down on that one. "It's a holiday—no naps!" they protested.

And so off we went to see "Fantasia" at the local cinema. Looking around, it was like Ralph Wilson Stadium on a bye week. There was one father and his little girl there and that was the extent of the audience. I began to feel sorry for myself, missing the camaraderie of family on such a day. But we were soon drawn to the music, color and style of the film and carried away to the land of imagination. We ended up talking about that movie for days around the dinner table.

Ever since, an important part of our pre-holiday preparation is scouting the movie house schedules, analyzing the movie reviews and taking note of the ratings. We vary the offerings. Sometimes it's an animated cartoon (to please the youngest), and as they got older, sometimes a chick flick (to please our daughter). Other times an action movie thrilled the guys. As for Mom, I was just happy to be there, content that the whole family is together for one more pleasant memory.

Our eight-year-old granddaughter has now added a generation and voice to our family outings. From our viewpoint, animated cartoons are becoming more sophisticated, designed to be adult-friendly as well as kid-friendly. We've also noticed we don't have the theater to ourselves any more. It's often filled to overflowing with large audiences on holiday afternoons.

This past Father's Day, we took in *Madagascar 3*, an animation that had the added attraction of being in 3-D. Some 3-Ds aren't worth the bother of putting on the special eyewear. This one was different—you were actually ducking that bright-colored bird careening toward your nose. Transported by the sound of beautiful voices singing beautiful music, many of us still sat there after the final scene when the credits started to roll. As the music continued, the audience, including my daughter and her daughter, began to sing too, everyone enjoying the impromptu karaoke. And then, suddenly, a man in the front row jumped out of his seat and began dancing, head bobbing and arms pumping to the beat, the silhouette of this joyful figure magnified on the movie screen. He bopped throughout the credit roll and when it, the music, and he came to a close, the rest of us gave him hearty applause.

A celebration of the spirit—what a great way to end the day.

November 2012

Words She Left Behind

"A little consideration,
a little thought for others,
makes all the difference."
Eeyore on a good day

When retiring from our church, our pastor received a copy of Dr. Seuss's *Oh, the Places You Will Go!* from the children in the congregation. It was presented to her at the retirement dinner jokingly referred to as the "last supper".

Soon after, having reached that stage when distant cities and mountains beckoned, Rev. Faith packed up her RV with the book and "Kitty" the cat and was on her way.

We miss her attributes—she was creative, funny and compassionate—but she did leave behind her sayings. Along with memories of potluck movie nights, bagpipes at Easter and amazing Bible studies, I still recall them, like the one that made me sit up straighter in the pew one Sunday.

"You have each other's backs," she said with conviction from the pulpit. It's not just a Sunday thing, she reminded us, getting to know the persons sitting beside you in church. You need to reach out to each other during the week, praying for them and checking in to see how they are doing. I had never heard clergy state that sentiment quite that way before. It was plain enough to stick in my head: "You have each other's backs."

This saying came alive when she made an announcement a week or so later, "Nora needs a ride for chemo treatment on Tuesday," she announced. "Who can do it?" and five hands shot up.

"Give them the benefit of the doubt." Rev. Faith emphasized that when helping the poor, give with a kind heart. Don't judge them because they look scruffy and sleep under a bridge. Everyone has a story, she said, and you don't know theirs. During our harsh winters, she stores gloves and hats in her car, handing them out to shivering persons lingering on street corners.

"It's not all about you." Before reading scripture during the service, she often prefaced it with: "Hebrew Scripture can be found in the front of the Bible and New Testament in the back." Long-time members queried her later: "Why are you telling us something so basic?" A pastor has to minister to all the people sitting in the pews, she explained. Some are from different or no church backgrounds; they need the guidance. No, indeed, it is not all about you....

"Choose not to be part of every argument you're invited to." This saying was a mouthful but it hit home. Two friends I love dearly haven't communicated with each other in years. Now when Elaine asks, "Have you heard from Cindy?" I keep the answer short, then change the subject.

"Yes, she sent a birthday card," I answer. "Say, how is Tom doing at college?" Rather than listen to still another hurtful remembrance, I turn down the invitation to take part in the drama.

This is the powerful thing about Rev. Faith's sayings—their meanings continue to evolve and add substance to the experiences I have every day.

One of her favorite characters was Eeyore, the bedraggled grey donkey in *Winnie the Pooh*. She pointed out that even though he was not a happy soul, and even a bit odd, his friends loved and accepted him just the way he was.

I have a few Eeyores in my own life. I will try hard to always have their backs, give them the benefit of the doubt, realize it is not all about me, and back out of arguments about who is right. All I can do is hope and pray that they do the same for me.

August 2017

My Favorite Hoard

*"So the writer who breeds
more words than he needs,
is making a chore
for the reader who reads."*
Theodor Seuss Geisel

I'm a "de-clutterer" and that means I am driven to toss out unused waffle irons along with undated pictures of unknown persons. On the other hand, as a writer, the things I produce the most—words—I hoard. They are like newborns, bursting forth with Lamaze-like heavy breathing and great spasms of pushing. And in my world, great rejoicing occurs.

Unless, of course, it doesn't.

Rejection slips underscore the futility of such difficult birth stories. Most are simply form letters with the usual, "Your manuscript does not meet the needs of our publication." Some have a softer edge like the one I received from a writer's magazine emanating from somewhere in Iowa. "I like this piece," the editor wrote, "but I don't love it." Velvety or not, it was still a "no".

Interviewing is a big part of the kind of non-fiction writing I am into. What I am looking for from the interviewee are quotes that pop off the page and catch the reader's attention. Sometimes I get so caught up in them myself, I lose my footing. One day, while reporting for the Chautauquan Daily, I conducted a phone interview with sex therapist and author "Dr. Ruth" Westheimer. My article would preview a lecture she was scheduled to make to the adults of the Institution. As I scrambled to write down the exact sexual terminology she was planning to use, she hesitated mid-sentence.

"Is this a family newspaper?" she asked. "Will these words be OK? Can you print them?" She stopped me in my tracks. "Perhaps not," I replied slowly. "No—yes, this is a family newspaper. Yes, of course, it is," I finally blurted. Why hadn't I thought of that? How unseemly if one of our Chautauquan children spied the article and asked, "Mom, what does this word mean?" Dr. Ruth changed course immediately—and words—bless her.

Sometimes a *reader* gets confused as to who said what in an article and then the *writer* is really in trouble. While reporting at The Telegraph, a daily in Ohio, I interviewed a marriage counselor about the techniques needed for a satisfying long-lasting relationship. My article appeared soon after with the headline: "Sex in Mid-Life." The next day, a colleague met me in the hallway. "Like I was telling my wife after reading your article," he related, "you said we should still be having sex, even at our age." He paused. "We had a fight about it. She said you're wrong."

"Oh, no!" I screamed in my head. But taking a deep breath, I explained calmly, "Those were not my words. They were the counselor's." It was hopeless. He wanted to have a discussion about his sex life there and then. He needed his very own Dr. Ruth.

Just for the record, I do write about subjects other than sex. For instance, in one "My View" for The Buffalo News, I penned an essay critical of restaurants lacking coat racks. One friend, reading my words to her breakfast club, reported back that they quite literally connected to my words. Dodging a rainstorm as they ran into the restaurant, with nowhere to hang their jackets, they were sitting uncomfortably in drenched clothing. They vented their frustration by banging their forks on the table and chanting, "We need a coat rack! We need a coat rack!"

Words—I love them, what can I say? They can fly back in my face and cause me grief, but they also render me joy when they inspire others. And though some of them will eventually end up in the trash, I am keeping the rest. They are my favorite hoard.

May 2018

Grandmas Worry

"It will be 'A Beautiful Tomorrow.'"
Mark Vidaver

OK, so I worry. Grandmas do that.

While our granddaughter was vacationing in Hawaii with relatives, a severe strain of winter flu had landed many Americans in hospitals. I chided myself that I was being over-dramatic when I began worrying about our favorite 14-year-old Isabella. Riding in my daughter's car that cold day in January, I relaxed when Christa reported that her daughter was having a great time in Paradise.

Mid-ride, her cell phone rang. Pulling over to the curb, she read the caller's name. "It's Isabella," she announced and put it on the speaker so I could hear, too. I was thrilled.

"Hello, sweetie, what's up?" my daughter asked.

"Mom, I don't want to worry you," Isabella answered. Then she paused. "But there's a missile headed for Hawaii."

"What?"

"Yes, Dad insisted I call you before you see it on TV."

"How do you know?"

"It came on our phones. Here, I'll read it to you, 'Emergency alert. Ballistic missile threat inbound to Hawaii. Seek immediate shelter. This is not a drill.'" Her voice was clear and steady.

We locked eyes as we both leaned closer to the dashboard. I could read Christa's mind. This is not real. This scenario could not be happening in real time.

"Grandma's here with me," my daughter said.

"Hi, Sweetheart," I said, louder than I needed to. "It's Grandma. Did everyone get that message?"

"Yes. We all got it on our phones." She still sounded amazingly calm. "What time is it there?" I asked.

"Eight in the morning. We're just getting up."

"Where are you?"

"In our room."

Starting to choke up, I nodded to my daughter to take over the conversation.

But before she could speak, tears ran down her face. We both began to cry and our teen so far away heard us.

"I didn't want to tell you, Mom, but Dad said I should," she said after a moment.

"No, that's OK," my daughter quickly answered, clearing her throat. "We would want to know. What will you do next?'

"Go to breakfast," Isabella answered, nonchalantly.

Pause on our end.

"But what will you do next?" her mom insisted.

"Go to breakfast," she again answered.

Go to breakfast? That seemed so ordinary, something they would do if a missile was not hurtling toward Hawaii. Shouldn't they all run immediately to a shelter?

I did not want the conversation to end. Would we ever talk to my granddaughter again? See her again?

We finally had to let her go. "We love you, we love you, we love you," we both said, pouring as much caring into the words as possible. I put my head down into my hands to wipe away tears and the irony of the situation hit me: I had been worried about the flu....

Quickly, Christa and I pulled ourselves together, drove to my home and ran to the television set. We listened to it for 30 terrifying minutes until the announcement came— there was no missile. An employee in a Hawaiian agency had pushed the wrong button. We were so drained, we could not cheer. Quietly, we hugged each other. Telephone calls were made.

I was so proud of my granddaughter's demeanor during that stressful time. I see now what a special young lady she has become. When faced with such a horrific emergency, Isabella was grace personified.

As for me, the worrier? Somehow there should be a lesson in this story for me. I worried about the flu and instead, dodged a missile. Erma Bombeck was right. "Worry is like a rocking chair," she said. "It gives you something to do but never gets you anywhere."

August 2018

Tennis Love

"Time you enjoyed wasting is not wasted time."
T.S. Eliot

Y-e-s-s, we know—Buffalo is a sports town. We cheer on our football and our hockey and our baseball teams with gusto—both inside and outside their venues. But there is another sport some of us still cling to. *Some* is the operative word here. Admittedly, we've found few other diehards.

I'm talking about tennis, a year-round favorite at the Vidaver's house.

Many of us recognize the names of the four Grand Slam tournaments played annually in the United States, England, Australia and France. But in our living room, on our TV, the lesser ones located in exotic locations like Dubai, Hong Kong, Shanghai, and Jamaica fill in the rest of the viewing hours.

All those years ago (54), one of the things that attracted me to my husband was the fact he liked tennis. No, actually, more like he *loved* tennis. A wonderful player, he even looked the part. He was tall and slim with a right arm stretching inches longer than his left. Obviously, a result of the multitude of serves pounded and shots returned on various courts in his birthplace, Southern California.

We hit it off because I was a tennis nut myself, having taught the sport at a Catskill summer camp while in college. I remember being outraged when a couple of teenagers who were talented players decided they would rather spend time at the stables than thwacking a tennis ball across the net. What were they thinking? Imagine choosing horseback riding over tennis...

Growing up in the Forest Hills neighborhood in Queens where the U.S. Open tournaments were held to great fanfare, I accept the fact that the antics of celebrities are ingrained in my psyche. Arthur Ashe with his graceful demeanor played off the likes of Jimmy Connors with his fan-busting enthusiasm and John McEnroe with his explosive courtside manner.

They fascinated me. I began seeking out public courts, slamming my balls against a concrete wall when I couldn't find a partner. I really worked at developing my backhand, my weakest shot. You have to remember, those were the days when we used only one hand on our racket to swing at our opponent's volleys. Whenever the two-handed grip came into style, I must have been dozing on the couch. Like a 119-mile serve bursting from Serena Williams, I did not see it coming. (I must admit, it still seems a little wimpy to me.)

Our daughter surprised us one year with a trip to the U.S. Open's newer Flushing Meadows Park. It was a wonderful visit. Still agile enough to climb into the upper, upper stands, we enjoyed soaking up the atmosphere. Andre Agassi was the star and made the day bright with his out-of-control shock of hair and neon tennis duds. If you remember, he was the one railing against the long-held traditional all-white dress codes required at England's Wimbledon. For sure, tennis has had its share of pioneers as well as rebels.

Scheduled for January 14, the Australian Open, in all its warm-weather glory, is a great way to begin 2019. The French Open takes place starting on Memorial Day, May 27, and beyond. July 2 brings us "Breakfast at Wimbledon" played at The All England Lawn Tennis Club when, in front of the TV, we eat strawberries with clotted cream like the Brits do. The U.S. Open begins August 27, runs for two weeks and includes the Labor Day weekend.

I don't know about y'all, but our plans for several holidays are already made for next year, thank you very much. You know where you can find us.

October 2018

The Gatekeepers

"The simple answer is to act."
Chinese fortune cookie

When the subject of church safety comes up, people focus on potential harm to innocent parishioners sitting in a Sunday worship service. The gatekeepers, on the other hand—the administrators and secretaries who are there to open the door to visitors—hold down the building by themselves for hours every week. What safety measures are in place for them?

Years past, I was that church secretary. My story begins with the day a stranger walked into my office with the outline of a gun clearly bulging beneath his shirt. Scary moment. I somehow notified the pastor who lived in the parsonage next door. He came over and dealt pleasantly with the man who was asking for a food handout from our pantry.

He received it, in a hurry. The pastor then walked him right to the door, making sure it was locked behind him. Turning to me, he said. "So much for a gun-free zone. Let's call the police."

At the area-wide church secretaries' meeting that month, the subject turned to safety in our churches. It soon became evident that we all had anxious moments when we were alone in the church building.

Those of us with food pantries noted the increased foot-traffic between the times the pantries were officially open. Did we turn anyone down who wanted food? Not likely.

We also had occasional transients who asked for gas money and sometimes lodging. These people were not known; they were telling stories the secretaries could not verify. We shared methods for screening visitors that we each used in our respective churches.

Sue, at her job, called through the outside locked door when she was alone in the church and didn't open it unless it was a person she knew. The disadvantage of that method? It was obvious to the visitor that she was the only one in the building.

Maxine had a monitor in her office showing her who was at the door, which she could not see from her vantage point. She spoke with the visitors through the intercom, then buzzed them in. When she had doubts, she asked them to call the next day and make an appointment. The disadvantage? When anyone comes through that door, it was often left unlocked.

Ann had a peephole in her door, but the visitor was only visible if they stood directly in front of it. This rarely happened. Also, she has never refused to open it, even for strangers. The disadvantage? Ann's conscience nudged her to keep unlocking the door.

None of these methods worked well and we were well aware of it.

Every secretary and administrator in a church needs a safety plan--they are in such a vulnerable position!

Church leaders should be diligent in making sure their valuable staff members are secure, safe and stress-free.

Another Voice
March 2018

The Mall as Town Square

"Let's take a walk, Chick."
Lois' dad, using her nickname

While I was growing up in New York City, my father and I often took long afternoon walks, always with a destination in mind. One of our favorites was a trek to the Queens County Courthouse. Sliding into seats in the back of a courtroom, who knew what mayhem we would hear about? We were up for it.

In my 20s, moving west to San Francisco, I met the man of my dreams. We spent our courtship walking all over that hilly terrain. No car, but that didn't matter—city folks walk; that's what we do. Next, we moved to the Chicago area where I spent five years walking, or let's say, blowing around that Windy City.

So coming to Western New York 35 years ago, we sought out a suburban home with urban-like perks, craving destinations we could stroll to, like a library, a bank, a bookstore and lots of restaurants.

We found them in a perfect location near the intersection of Maple Road and Niagara Falls Boulevard.

In reality, the draw was Boulevard Mall, just blocks away with its many attractions. In those years, at the record store, I was the one sorting through albums hunting for Broadway show tunes. My teenage kids, in the meantime, hung out at the arcade with their friends.

My husband took up the habit of walking to and through the shopping center for an almost-daily jaunt. We called him "The Mayor of the Mall," as he stopped to chat up the kiosk vendors and the landscapers who added beauty to the place.

It was natural then, that when we were blessed with a granddaughter, we introduced her to this lively destination. Every Wednesday, Grandma and Grandpa strolled her there, then unleashed her to dash around the play area nonstop. Capping off the visit with a ride on the Carousel with Grandpa, Grandma stood by, waving. The short ride home was followed by a nap (for everybody).

The years soared by. Our latest venture with the now-teenager Isabella was to cruise the stores for that special Confirmation dress. Yes, we found a beauteous one at Macy's.

During the last few months, several family members have discovered a new treat. We attend the monthly poetry readings at "The Screening Room." What a wonderful way to spend an evening—listening to creative folks at the mic.

Sitting on a bench watching the crowds is still a favorite pastime and we usually do see and greet a couple of friends and neighbors. "Who did you meet?" is always the question when any one of us comes back from a shopping trip.

There was one time when I really did not want to meet anyone. Having recently started a diet program, I ran into a friend and told him about it. After we parted, I decided to splurge one last time on a chocolate-laden ice cream sundae featured at the Food Court. Hiding my guilty pleasure, I found a table behind a potted bush.

I was literally crouching, filling my mouth with a heaping spoonful of whipped cream, when I heard his laughter.

"Oh, hiding behind a plant, are we?" he called to me. "Eating ice cream???"

I actually blushed. You can't get away with much in my mall. There are friends skulking everywhere.

The Boulevard Mall has changed through the years. Indeed, we have, too. We don't walk the three blocks to it anymore. We drive our car but still enjoy the time inside. The Food Court is gone but dinners at Fridays with our family are always a treat.

It has been a good neighbor and remains a great destination for us all.

April 2019

'Largo' on the Massey

*"The reason I like to play the organ is that
I like to make the really big sounds."*
Jared's sharing with children at Chautauqua

I once had the temerity to ask Jared Jacobsen if we could write a book together. Very kindly, as was his way, he turned me down.

As a Chautauquan Daily reporter for four summers, my assignments included the Department of Religion. Jared, Worship Coordinator and Organist at Chautauqua Institution, was an important part of my beat. Our weekly interviews brimmed over with his joyous spirit as he filled my recorder with memorable quotes and anecdotes.

There was every indication that at the age of 70, he would continue to inspire visitors for years with his mastery at the Massey Memorial Organ and his amazing choral direction. So it was unbelievable to receive news days after this summer season closed, that Jared Jacobsen had perished in a car crash in Ohio on the afternoon of August 27. Those who knew him are heart-broken, seeking solace with Facebook and email exchanges.

Though there is no book, I have saved several of the articles we worked on together. Enough of my words. Most of the following are Jared's.

To begin, the Massey Organ celebrated its 100th Anniversary in 2007. In the article about this occasion, Jared related this story: "Once, during a boring sermon (not at Chautauqua!), I was contemplating the need for a new pair of organ shoes and determined that I had played several hundred million notes with my then-12-year-old pair. This summer when I think of the billions of notes that have been played by the century-old pipes of the Massey Memorial Organ, I am awestruck by the history they have seen on this platform—speeches by poets, preachers, and presidents and, of course, a thousand 'Largos'.

"I have been privileged to play several million of these notes myself," he went on, "and every time I put hands and feet to the keys, the largest and most complex of instruments, the same thing happens: the Massey takes me into a zone where mechanisms vanish away, and music-making pours out of me without conscious thought, filling the Amphitheater with roars and whispers.

"To my parents, who brought me as a five-year-old child, I owe an enormous debt of gratitude, which I hope to repay in some small part by sharing my love of this extraordinary organ with present and future Chautauquans. Do I have the best job in the world? Undoubtedly!"

His mention of "Largo" brings us to another article, titled "The 'Largo' Tradition." Sacred Song Services on Sunday evenings have been concluded with Handel's oratorio since organist Henry Vincent played it for the Massey Memorial Organ's first program in 1907.

"It's a tiny fragment of a completely obscure oratorio based on the Xerxes story," Jared explained. "It's not even a religious thing. The original text was about nature." Somehow, during the years, it was adopted and now, he said, "We revere 'Largo' here."

In the season's last edition of August 27 & 28 in 2005, Jared grew reflective as he walked his beloved dog, Pierrot.

"As I came down lower Forest and saw the lake in front of me, it was just one of those perfect Chautauqua days," he remembered. "I said to the dog, 'What would happen if we just stayed here and didn't go back to San Diego?' and he sort of looked at me and wagged his tail and kept on going."

Then Jared shared how much he relished coming back to a place where everything was exactly the same as he remembered it. "That's the thing people long for more than anything else at Chautauqua," he said, "that it be a stable place in a very unstable world."

September 2019

Community Brightens our Lives

"The solution to alone-ness is not more solitude,
but companionship and community. "
Robert Fulghum

There's something about community that our family leans into. We seem to seek out folks we can hang with, either at summer camp or for weekly breakfast dates.

This way of life, I believe, all began one morning during our Ohio days. I woke up to hear my groggy husband Mike muttering, "I don't know, I think I'm getting a little bored with our lives." Oops, that was certainly a splash of cold-water-in-the-face, wake-up-fast kind of moment.

Rather than panic, we talked about it. It turns out, we both felt like we were becoming inward-looking. Ready to do something to lift us out of a funk, we went on a Marriage Encounter (ME) weekend. Its slogan, "Making a good marriage, great" and following its 20-minutes a day program of intense dialogue, helped our relationship blossom. We found ourselves in a community of like-minded couples, meeting weekly in each other's homes.

When we were asked to lead weekends, other ME couples watched our children while we flew off to Connecticut and Indiana. Our kids soon had lots of new aunts, uncles, and cousins, learning to trust friends who became like family. It was a wholesome environment for all of us. We still often talk with joy about our ME days.

The Bruderhof was another interesting community experience for our family. It was so very different from our everyday lives. Bruderhof is a lifestyle that practices the example of the first Christian church.

Spending two weeks in that rural Pennsylvania commune, it was as though we had parachuted into another planet. Families as well as single men and women who gathered around the dinner meal ate in silence (the children ate separately). Background music was provided by an orchestra softly playing the classics. Surprisingly, this concert was not applauded. Everything done in the Bruderhof is "to the glory of God," not to plump up egos. Unsigned paintings lining the walls underscored this philosophy.

Although there was no charge for visitors, it was expected that we would work for our room and board, placed in the area where the community needed us. Mike was assigned to building toys in the Community Playthings workshop. I was delegated to the laundry. Humility not being my strong suit, I protested. "I do not like ironing," I stated. Whoa, I cringe even writing that sentence. I really didn't get it at the beginning. In that atmosphere, we learned to think of others, not ourselves. My partner in the laundry, for instance, had earned a master's degree in biology and probably didn't like steaming shirts either but she wasn't whining. It's a memory I bring to mind when I begin to feel uppity.

Recently, we began looking for fellowship in a different way. Community lunches and dinners have sprung up around us and we find ourselves attending them. Put on by local churches, they attract diners coming from near and far to share a meal. After dropping in at the same location several times, we end up making new acquaintances. We always search for one regular, for instance, who reminds us of the friendly character "Norm" in the Cheers' gang on the old TV sitcom.

Each venue offers a different vibe. One finishes up with a hymn-sing and short meditation. Still another sports its motto on a big sign at the entrance: "No preachin', just eatin'."

Looking back, when we realized that we had to stop thinking that we are all we need, we reached outside of our comfort zone for community. It certainly enhanced our family's life story. Which, as you can surmise, is still in the process of being written.

November 2019

Trivial Nonsense

"What year was the Erie Canal completed?"
Trivia Game question

Years ago, my mother and brother drove here from Long Island to visit for a few days. We were pressed to come up with entertainment ideas. Mom wasn't walking well, so sightseeing was out. Television was not an option: she would rather talk than be quiet. In preparation, I created a Vidaver-style Trivia Game. It was designed so the questions included Mom's favorite things--New York City and her love of all things *sugar*. We sat in our living room in front of a roaring fire and began.

"What is the most popular bakery in New York?" was the first one. Not a difficult one for her. "Entenmanns," she answered, with a "Who wouldn't know that?" expression. "OK, what are New York's most popular cookies?" was the second. "Black and whites, of course." Our mother looked triumphant. My brother and I didn't stand a chance.

Ever since, Trivia games have become one of our favorite go-to family activities. When our granddaughter was old enough to participate, the challenge was to field questions we could all answer. Finding a game called "Brain Quest: 1,500 Questions and answers to Challenge the Mind" put us all in the mindset that we were 10 years old and attending fourth grade. We tried answering these mindbenders: (1) Who belonged to the League of Five Nations: the Iroquois or the Sioux? (2) Which body of water has the most earthquakes along its edges? (3) Name the planet closest to the sun. (4) Geese teach their young to fly south before winter comes. True or false? Hmm, not so easy.

There are other ways we end a family dinner. Sometimes it is with a rousing game of Scrabble, though we don't always follow the official rules. During the latest one, I triumphantly put down the word "flirty" for mucho points. A couple of turns later someone noticed the letter "t" was missing. To my gleeful family, I lost a turn, then watched my score for "fliry" (sic) erased. It was all downhill from there.

But...Trivia still reigns. These days one of us goes online and types in an up-coming holiday followed by the words "Trivia Games". Needing all the hints we can get, we look for those with multiple-choice questions. On Memorial Day, these questions might come up: (5) What were decorated in remembrance of this day? Tombs of fallen Union soldiers; Cemeteries of family, or State Capitals? (6) What is one of the longest standing traditions held in conjunction with Memorial Day since 1911? Arizona Rodeo Days, Washington DC Apple Blossom Festival or Indianapolis 500?

The ones with no choices are the toughest. For a 50th birthday celebration, we tackled the theme of "Music of the 80s." (7) Which former child star appeared in Little Johnny Jones in the 1980s? and (8) Stevie Wonder was given the keys to which city in recognition of his talents in 1984?

For reading and writing buffs, there is a "Literary Trivia" book chock full of Q and A's: These first lines come from what books? (9) "When he was nearly 13, my brother Jeb got his arm badly broken at the elbow" and (10) "'Christmas won't be Christmas without any presents,' grumbled Jo, lying on the rug."

Don't know the answers? Here they are for your reading pleasure: (1) The Iroquois; (2) Pacific; (3) Mercury; (4) False (Migration is an inborn behavior); (5) Cemeteries of family; (6) Indianapolis 500; (7) Donny Osmond; (8) Detroit; (9) *To Kill a Mockingbird*; (10) *Little Women.*

This Brain Quest question won't strain your brain. Which is a body of salt water: Lake Erie or the Gulf of Mexico? For sure, we all know that answer.

January 2020

Epilogue

This book ends with a wannabe "My View". I wrote it on the day New York State Gov. Andrew Cuomo hosted his last daily TV press conference. A coronavirus pandemic has ravaged our country from mid-March, with millions of patients as well as thousands of deaths. Andrew chiseled out a slogan for New Yorkers designed to sustain us through a long lockdown. For 111 straight days, he brought into our living room a sense of purpose. Not every citizen had that reaction, so controversy arose.

Therefore, it is our family's decision not to publish this essay in our local newspaper. This one is just for you....

New York Tough

"I'd rather be known as **Strong.** *"*
Lois Vidaver

I am New York tough, smart, united, disciplined and loving.

Tough must come in my DNA because I was raised in Queens, N.Y. From what I garner on TV, that seems to a center of toughness. When I grew up there, attending Richmond Hill High School, it had a genteel feel to it. We were church kids, many of us, attending choir rehearsals, then stopping at a deli for limburger cheese on pumpernickel with a slice of onion on top. A special treat was gathering at Jahn's Ice Cream Parlor where we shared a Queens Stinger sundae for 65 cents. "Fine French Ice Cream Since 1897" boasts the menu. Tough? Naah, not then, but I am willing to claim it now if it fits in with beating back this coronavirus pandemic. Yeah, I'll take 'tough.'

Smart? I'll take that one, too. Smart enough to come of age in New York City when they gifted residents with a free ride to four years at a city college. There was zero tuition and no charge for textbooks at Hunter College until maybe my senior year when there was a nominal fee (eight dollars) for something or another. We paid a hefty price, though, in the lack of interesting coeds. At the time, it was an all-girls school.

I've tried to bring that smartness to this pandemic. T'ain't easy. Deemed vulnerable early on by doctors and just about everyone else in our world, (especially our children), my husband and I have stayed home. Cancelling doctors' appointments, we skipped exercise classes and physical therapy as well. March 11 was our last social outing and we vow to stay in until several weeks past Phase Four. We think it's smart to keep others safe as well as ourselves.

United? Yes, I feel very much a part of the Western New York community right now. We are all in the same boat, trying to navigate a swift current and steer our way to safety. Reaching out to friends more than usual, phone calls are being made, notes posted and chats over the fence with our neighbors treasured. If I detect someone is feeling restless in this new reality, I mail them a Marmaduke cartoon or Pickles comic strip. Later, when they telephone, though I can't see the smile on their face, I can hear it.

Disciplined? Yes. Scheduling three projects a day, my favorite is sifting through boxes of memorabilia. One gem discovered was a tattered 1945 newspaper clipping reporting on my brother's heroics during World War II. As a Marine, Roy earned a Bronze Star and Purple Heart. Along with the article, I found his hand-drawn card postmarked Okinawa with a P.S. plea, "Lois, please write back!" Here's hoping my nine-year-old self had the discipline to do just that.

Loving? You betcha. Bonding in this common cause, Mike and I make time for each other, reading old love letters from the 60s, watching long ago tennis tournaments (Don't they have an expiration date?) on TV and skyping Sunday dinners with those we cannot hug. Our church elders, bless them, provide three events each week which draw us to the computer.

One day recently, our doorbell rang. There, on the sidewalk, was our bagpiper friend, brightening up the day by playing a lilting melody just for us. Well, OK, for our neighbors as well. (It is a bagpipe after all.) Now I would call that a gift of love.

Yes, I own up to it: whether from birth or living through a pandemic, I am New York Tough. *(Truth be told, I'd rather be known as* Strong, *but right now? I'll take* Tough.*)*

June 2020

About the Author

New York City native **Lois Vidaver** graduated from the Hunter College creative writing program. She began her literary career as an assistant editor at Henry Holt Publishing Company on Madison Avenue.

At the age of 44, she earned her first newspaper byline by joining the staff of The Telegraph in Painesville, Ohio. As both a feature and religion writer, she won awards from the United Press International Ohio Newspaper Awards, the Associated Press Society of Ohio, Ohio Newspaper Women's Association, The National School Boards Association and the National League of American Pen Women.

Lois was, as well, a staff writer for the Niagara Gazette and the Chautauquan Daily at the Chautauqua Institution. She lives in the Town of Tonawanda, N.Y. with her family.

Celebrating her 40th year in journalism, publication of this book brings great joy to her heart!

Made in the USA
Coppell, TX
17 October 2023